MINDS

A Poetry Collection of Her-Story

Lorraine Estelle Bills

MINDS

S.H.E. PUBLISHING, LLC

For information contact:
www.shepublishingllc.com | info@shepublishingllc.com
Cover and Title Page Design by Nabin Karna
ISBN: 978-1-964061-06-1
First Edition: June 2024
10 9 8 7 6 5 4 3 2 1

CONTENTS

MINES

MINES

QUIET LAY

Dedicated to Milford Dunn

AS I PREPARE MYSELF,
TO GIVE TO YOU
IMAGINATION RUNS WILD,
THE THINGS TO DO
TO SATISFY YOU,
IS THE ULTIMATE GOAL
TO HAVE YOUR LOVE,
BE MINE TO HOLD
I'LL COME TO YOU,
PURE EACH TIME LOVE IS MADE
AND PLACE MY BODY DOWN,
FOR A QUIET LAY
TAKE ME IN YOUR ARMS,
AND PLACE YOURSELF UPON ME
AND WE'LL CARESS BOTH BODIES
WITH MAJESTY
AND AS WE DRIFT INTO PARADISE,
EXPERIENCING THE LOVE
MORE THAN TWICE
TO PLACE YOU IN AN ATMOSPHERE,

MINES

WHERE YOU'LL FEEL IT TOO
I'LL DO EVERYTHING,
I MUST DO
AND UNTIL WE ACHIEVE,
THE CLIMAX TO ECSTASY
WE LAY STROKING EACH OTHER,
UNTIL THERE'LL BE
AND AS WE MAKE,
THAT MOMENT COME DOWN
JUST KEEP STROKING,
MAKE NO SOUND
WE JOIN TOGETHER,
OUR LOVE A SILENT JOY IS FELT
AND INTO EACH OTHERS LOVE,
THE BODIES MELT.
AHH!!!

A CRUSH ON YOU

YOU LIVE THE FAST LIFE,
ALWAYS ON THE GO
BUT THERE'S ONE THING,
YOU REALLY SHOULDN'T KNOW
I WATCH YOU PASS ME BY,
I LOOK IN YOUR FACE
DOWN THE STREET AS YOU CRUISE,
MY HEART STARTS TO RACE
I SEE THE WAY YOU LOOK AT ME,
WHEN I'M ON THE STREET
I TOLD YOU, MY ATTRACTION,
WHEN WE FIRST MEET
MY FEELINGS FOR YOU,
TO YOU I MUST REVEAL IT
IT COMES IN MY DREAMS,
AND I CAN'T CONCEAL IT
EACH TIME I LOOK INTO YOUR EYES,
I SEE THE PASSION REACH YOU
NOW FROM THIS STEP TO THE NEXT,
WHAT SHALL I DO
TO SAY A MAN

MINES

THAT LIVES A FAST LIFE HAS NO LOVE
BUT I WANT TO CHALLENGE THE THEORY
IF NOT TO BE YOUR LOVE,
OR LOVER, FOR FOREVER AND A DAY
MAYBE JUST A DAY
I WANT TO BE WITH YOU,
BUT I DON'T KNOW HOW
IN MY HEART,
I CAN FEEL THE HEAT NOW

WHAT

WHAT THIS IS:
IS THE BEGINNING OF MY STORY
THE VERY MOMENT I SAW YOU,
I KNEW I LOVED YOU
AS I WATCHED YOU,
MY MIND FANTASIZED
ABOUT MAKING LOVE
YOU GATHERED ME UP INTO YOUR ARMS,
GENTLY PRESSING YOUR LIPS UPON MINE
AND SUDDENLY,
A VERY WARM FEELING
TAKES US OVER
AS I LOOK AT YOU,
I SEE THE SAME IN YOUR EYES
AND EACH TIME I SEE YOU,
I FEEL THE SAME WAY
WHAT IS THE BEGINNING
OF EACH AND EVERY DAY
TO SEE THE SUNRISE

WHERE

WHERE I PLAN FOR THIS FEELING
TO GO IS A NEVERENDING LIMIT
WITH NO PRESSURES,
I'LL BE THE WOMAN THAT IS THERE,
WHEN YOU FEEL THE NEED.
ALL I ASK IS THAT
YOU SHARE A PART OF YOUR LIFE,
AND LOVE WITH ME
AND WHERE YOU ARE,
IS WHERE MY LOVE
AND THOUGHTS WILL BE
SO SHARE MY BED,
SHARE MY HEART,
AND PLEASE TAKE ALL THE LOVE
AND I'LL TAKE YOUR LOVE
AND SAVE IT AS IF IT'S A PRECIOUS JEWEL
AND SPEND IT WITH THE RICHES OF THIS,
THAT THE WORLD POSSESS

WHEN

WHEN OUR HEARTS APART,
LOVE WILL LIVE WITH US
I WOULD NEVER FORGET NOR REGRET
THE LOVE AND WORLD WE SHARED
SO WHEN THE TIME COMES
FOR YOU TO LEAVE ME,
I SHALL NOT BE BITTER
I SHALL REMAIN STRONG,
FOR I KNOW IN MY HEART IT MUST BE
FOR THIS WILL BRING YOU CLOSER TO ME
IT IS APPARENT THAT I AM WEAK,
NOT SO WEAK THAT I'LL RUN
WHEN THINGS GET TOUGH
TO LOVE YOU REGARDLESS,
WHEN ITS AGAINST ME
WHEN YOU'RE WITH ME
I WANT TO HOLD YOU
THERE JUST ISN'T ENOUGH TIME TO DO
ALL OF THE THINGS YOU WANT TO DO,
ONCE YOU FIND THEM

WHY

TO LEARN WHAT IT IS TO BE LOVED
A LOVE THAT WE BOTH KNOW IS GIVEN
BUT LIKE THE APPLE THAT FIRST TEMPTED ADAM AND EVE,
IT'S THAT SAME MYSTERIOUS FEELING,
WE NOW PERCEIVE YOU ARE THE MAN
TO OPEN MY WORLD,
TO EXPAND MY KNOWLEDGE OF LOVE
WHY IS THE QUESTION,
THAT ALWAYS SEEKS WISDOM
WHY IS THE GRASS GREEN,
THE SKY BLUE
WHY DO WE LOVE MORE THAN ONCE
BUT IT DOESN'T CHANGE
THE WAY I FEEL ABOUT YOU

HOW

HOW:
ANYTIME
ANYWHERE
AS LONG AS WE BOTH NEED
AND WANT IT
SO IT SHALL BE GIVEN,
SO IT SHALL BE DONE

LOVING

TO BE IN LOVE IS FINE AND GRAND
YOU HOLD THE WORLD IN THE PALM OF YOUR HANDS
HOLDING EACH OTHER SAYING "I LOVE YOU"
AND FOREVER MY LOVE, WILL REMAIN TRUE
CRY FOR THE JOY, YOU MUST FEEL
ALL THIS LOVE, AND ITS REAL
MAKING PLANS, TO STAY TOGETHER
PROMISING NOT TO LEAVE EACH OTHER NEVER
WHEN I LOOK INTO YOUR EYES, ALL I CAN SEE
IS THE LOVE I HOLD FOR YOU, INSIDE OF ME

ALONE

THERES NO ONE LEFT, FOR ME TO SEE
AND NOW I'M ALONE, MEANT TO BE
I CANNOT CRY, BECAUSE I WAS WRONG
MY DISTINATION, NO LONGER PROLONG
EVEN STILL, I WISH TO HOLD YOU
AND HEAR YOU SAY, I LOVE YOU TOO
AND FOR ME THIS EMPTINESS, IS HARD TO BEAR
LOST AND ALONE; DO YOU CARE?
I CAN'T CHANGE THE PAST, AND THE MISTAKES I'VE MADE
NOW THIS HURT I HAVE, I'LL GLADLY TRADE
I HATE MYSELF FOR WHAT I'VE DONE
THE PRICE YOU PAY, WHEN YOU HURT SOMEONE
SO TRY TO SHARE THE PAIN I FEEL
AND TELL MYSELF, IT WASN'T REAL

COME AND GO

WHEN I LOOK OUT THE WINDOW,
I SEE A BEAUTIFUL COLOUR
THE NATURE OUTSIDE SHOWS HOW I FEEL
THE SKY IS BLUE, TO CONTRAST MY MOOD
I LOOK AROUND, AND YOU'RE NOT THERE
YOU COME AND GO, IN MY LIFE
EVERYTIME THIS HAPPENS,
I LOSE A PART OF MYSELF TO YOU
I'VE YET TO UNDERSTAND,
JUST WHAT IT IS I AM DOING HERE
WHEN ALL I WANT TO DO,
IS LAY IN YOUR ARMS AND MAKE LOVE FOREVER
BUT FOREVER NEVER COMES,
AND THEN
YOU ARE GONE.

FANTASY

DEEP IN THE WOODS,
ON A MOONLITE NIGHT
WE'RE ALL ALONE,
AND IT FEELS SO RIGHT
YOU MAKE LOVE WITH PASSION AND PAIN,
STROKING ME SOFTLY AGAIN AND AGAIN
IT FEELS SO GOOD BEING WITH YOU
AND WHEN YOU MAKE LOVE THE WAY YOU DO
ITS BEAUTIFUL TO HAVE THAT ECSTASY
BURSTING DEEP DOWN INSIDE OF ME
HAVING YOUR ARMS AROUND ME,
TO HOLD ME TIGHT
ALL BECAUSE OF YOU,
I MADE IT THROUGH THE NIGHT
YOU GAVE ME SOMETHING, NEEDED SO BAD
EXPOSING FEELINGS, I DIDN'T KNOW I HAD
IF LOVING YOU WAS WRONG,
DON'T LET ME KNOW
ONCE ISN'T ENOUGH,
AND I CAN'T LET IT GO

MISUNDERSTANDINGS

WE FIGHT AND FUSS ABOUT THIS OR THAT
TIL WE LOSE WHAT IS ACCOMPLISHED,
AND SET OURSELVES BACK
I DON'T NEED AN OUTSIDE LIFE,
WHEN YOU PROCLAIMED ME AS BEING YOUR WIFE
IT'S HARD TO GET YOU TO UNDERSTAND,
THAT THERE IS NO OTHER
WE'RE BECOMING ENEMIES INSTEAD OF LOVERS
I TELL THEM TO STAY AWAY,
DON'T KNOCK ON MY DOOR,
THOSE DAYS ARE GONE AND THERE IS NO MORE
BUT HOW DO YOU GET A JEALOUS PERSON TO SEE,
THAT THERS ONLY ME FOR YOU, AND YOU FOR ME
YOU MAKE ME SO ANGRY,
AND I'LL SAY THINGS I DON'T MEAN,
THEN I'LL TELL YOU TO SPLIT THE SCENE
BUT DEEP DOWN MY HEART DOESN'T WANT YOU TO LEAVE,
I WANT YOU TO KNOW THAT YOU'RE ALL I NEED
SO TRY NOT TO JUDGE ME, AND PUT ME ON TRIAL,
THEN HANG MY HEART OUT FOR A WHILE
I'M ONLY A WOMAN DOING THE BEST I CAN,
TO BE ABLE TO HANDLE A HELL OF A MAN

SIN CITY

WE RIDE AS BROTHERS
WE RIDE AS ONE
WE TRUST IN EACH OTHER
TIL NOON'S DAY SUN
WE HONOR AND PROTECT
DEVOTED TO OUR OWN
DON'T STEP IN OUR SHOES
TIL YOU'RE A MAN,
FULL SIZE GROWN
WEARING BLACK LEATHER
WITH DISCIPLE ON OUR BACK
RAISE HEADS HIGH
TO THE LEADER OF THE PACK
WE'RE BROTHERS UNITED
CONQUERED BY NONE
SO BE WARNED,
WE HAVE NO PITY
FOR THERE IS NO ESCAPE
FROM THIS SIN CITY

YOU'RE NOT ALONE

WHEN I PASS BY YOU,
I CAN ONLY SAY "HELLO"
YOU ALWAYS SEEM TO BE DEEP IN THOUGHT,
WHERE MINDS ARE,
HOW FAR DOES IT GO
DO YOU THINK ABOUT THE LOVE,
YOU MIGHT HAVE SOUGHT
YOU HIDE YOURSELF BEHIND DARK GLASSES
BUT I SEE THE LONELINESS, Y
OU FEEL IN YOUR EYES,
AS THOSE FILLINGS PASSES
TODAY I SAW YOU, YOU SEEMED SO ALONE
TIME WILL BRING BACK THE HAPPINESS,
YOU'VE ONCE KNOWN
I SEE IN YOUR FACE,
THE TEARS YOU MAY NEVER SHED
LOVE WILL LIVE FOREVER,
LET THE PAST BE DEAD
YOU'RE NOT ALONE, IS WHAT I SAY TO YOU
BECAUSE I SOMETIMES FEEL THAT SAME WAY TOO

MY FOREVER VALENTINE

I GIVE YOU MY LOVE
I PLEDGE ALWAYS
TO BE IN YOUR CORNER
TO GIVE OF MYSELF
AND BESTOW TO YOU
MY TRUST, FAITH,
AND UNDERSTANDING
AS I LAY TO REST,
THE MAN SHARING THIS
WHAT GOD UNITED
NO ONE WILL PUT IT UNDER
TOGETHER WE WILL PROSPER
AND BUILD STRENGTH
TOGETHER THERE IS NO TRIBULATIONS
WE CAN'T WITHSTAND
BECAUSE OUR LOVE
AND FOUNDATION IS SOLID.

WINTER

A WINTER LOVE
CAME TO SAY
I SHARE WITH YOU
THIS GOD GIVEN DAY
TO BE MY LOVE,
TOMORROW NEVER ENDS
GONE BACK TO YESTERDAY
TO HAVE LOVE AGAIN
WINTER LOVE
KEEP ME WARM
HOLD ME TIGHT
TODAY'S THE BEGINNING
OF LONG ENDLESS NIGHTS.

WATCHING YOU WATCHING ME

I SEE YOU WATCHING ME
AS I'M WATCHING YOU
YOU TURN YOUR HEAD
AT A SECONDS GLANCE,
BUT STILL I SEE
I WATCH YOU STARE AT ME
AS I PASS YOU BY
I FEEL YOUR EYES
AS I CONFRONT YOU,
YOUR EYES TELL A STORY
OF WONDER AND LUST
I KNOW BECAUSE
I LOOK INTO THEM
I SEE THE TRUTH BEHIND THEM
I TOLD YOU AT FIRST INTRODUCTION
THAT I WAS ATTRACTED TO YOU
WHEN I SAID IT,
I SAW YOUR ATTRACTION TOO
THE MORE YOU FIGHT

MINES

THE STRONGER IT GETS
THATS WHY YOU EXPRESS
A BOLD DENIAL TO MAKE IT BAD
I SEE IT IN MY AWAKEN FANTASY
LOOKING INTO YOUR EYES
AND IN MY DREAMS
MY DREAMS ALWAYS OFTEN COME TRUE
HOW ABOUT YOU?

NIGGERS I KNOW

THE NIGGERS I KNOW
THINK THEY'RE SLICK
WALKING AROUND ALL DAY,
JUST HOLDING THEIR DICK
HE THINKS HE'S A SLY FOX ON A DESERT
WHEN ALL ALONG,
HE'S A WALKING BUZZARD
DROPPING BABIES BY THE LOAD
HE THINKS HE'S KING OF ALL BEINGS
WHEN HE GET HALF BLOWED
CALLING WOMEN BITCHES BEHIND THEIR BACK
THINKING HE'S BIG, DRIVING AN UNAFFORDABLE CADILLAC
THE NIGGERS I KNOW DON'T HAVE THEM ALL
TRYING TO SCREW EVERY WOMAN
BECAUSE HE HAS BAT AND BALL
THEY WOULD JUMP DOWN YOUR BACK AT THE WORD "GO"
THEIR PRINCIPLES AND MORAL
ARE TOO DAMN LOW
START A CONVERSATION AND BEFORE YOU'RE THROUGH
THAT SAME DAMN NIGGER WILL START TELLING YOU

RICHES

TAKE AWAY ALL THE MATERIAL THINGS
THE WORLD OFFERS
TAKE THE BAD AND GIVE IT TO THE BAD
LET THE WORLD BE AT PEACE WITH ITSELF
GIVE ME ALL THE TREASURES OF LOVE SO PURE
LET ME BE ABLE TO GIVE BACK THAT LOVE WITH WARMTH
FILL THE WORLD WITH RICHES AND GOOD
ALWAYS IN LOVE AND NEVER UNSURE
PAY THE PRICE FOR HAPPINESS
IT'S AFFORDABLE TO ALL
AND TURN LOVE INTO MONEY
AND SPEND UNTIL IT'S ALL GONE
WHEN THE EARTH DRIES OUT THE SUN
CHERISH GOOD FAITH
IN ONLY ONE WAY
KEEPING YOUR HEAD TO THE SKY AND PRAY
PRAY THAT THE SUN SHINES,
THE TREES BLOW, BIRDS SING
PRAY FOR THE GOOD OF EVERYTHING

ANOTHER YEAR

THIS IS ANOTHER YEAR THAT HAS GONE BY
I HAVE NO ONE TO LOVE
AND NO ONE TO LOVE ME
IT'S HARD AND IT'S LONELY,
WHEN I'M USE TO HAVING SOMEONE
PAST RELATIONSHIPS COME BACK,
BUT WHY?
IS IT TO PUNISH ME
FOR THE LOVE THEY ONCE HAD
SHOWING ME THAT I WAS WRONG
IN MY JUDGMENT
IF SO, THEY NEED NOT RETURN
LONELINESS CAN'T KILL
SO LEAVE ME ALONE
HERE I AM DYING INSIDE MYSELF,
I SAY BE STRONG
SURVIVE, SO WHY DO I FEEL
SO WEAK AND DEFIED

HEART TO HEART

HOW BIG OF A FOOL ARE YOU?
CONSTANTLY GIVING
AND IT BREAKS YOUR HEART IN TWO
YOU'RE ALWAYS GETTING ME HURT
CAN'T YOU SEE YOU CAN'T SURVIVE WITHOUT ME
STOP GIVING ME AWAY AS IF I'M A GIFT
TO THIS MAN YOU FEEL,
A NEED TO BE WITH
BESIDES,
HE'S MARRIED
AND HE DOESN'T NEED YOU FOOL
SO STOP BEING LIKE A TEENAGER IN HIGH SCHOOL
BUT I LOVE HIM NO MATTER WHAT YOU SAY
THAT'S WHY I FEEL THE NEED
TO ACT THIS WAY
MARRIED,
WELL HE CAN HAVE HIS WIFE
I WANT HIM AS A PART OF MY LIFE
SO, I'M SORRY HEART IF I HURT YOU
BUT I KNOW, I HURT ME TOO.

YESTERDAY, TODAY, AND TOMORROW

YESTERDAY,
I THOUGHT ALL LOVE HAS GONE FROM ME
THERE WOULD NEVER BE ANYONE, FOR ME
YESTERDAY, DESTROYED BY NO LOVE
TORMENTED BY ILLUSION OF LOSING
I WALK ALONE FEELING NOTHING
TODAY,
I FEEL BLESSED TO HAVE SOMEONE IN MY LIFE
YOU'VE FILLED THAT EMPTINESS IN MY HEART
TODAY, I'M NOT AFRAID TO LOVE AGAIN; TAKE CHALLENGES
REFUSING TO BACK THAT BAG DOWN:
NO MATTER HOW MUCH TIME WE HAVE
IT REALLY ISN'T TIME ENOUGH, BUT THERE'S ALWAYS
TOMORROW,
FILLED WITH THOUGHTS OF YOU
AS LONG AS THERE IS YOU, LIFE WILL FILL WITH
TOMORROW, WILL NEVER BE AFRAID TO TELL
"WILL LOVE FOR ALL TOMORROWS, WE'LL HAVE?"

WHERE WE BELONG

SUMMER SONG BLOW SOFT AND SWEET
PLACING WINGS BENEATH MY FEET
FLOAT ME UP TO THE WORLD "PARADISE"
A WORLD WHERE LOVE
NEVER THINKS TWICE
TELL ME YOU LOVE ME FORE;
YOU KNOW I BELIEVE THIS LAND OF PARADISE
WE'LL NEVER LEAVE
DRINK WINE WITH ME, DANCE BY MOONLIGHT
UNDER THE STARY MOONLIGHT NIGHT
WE'LL DINE ON FRUIT AND HERBS
SEEKING ECSTASY BEYOND WORDS
KISSING YOU TIL WILD PASSIONS FLOW
GIVING LOVE, LIFES YET TO KNOW
WHEN IN A BLUE MOONLITE NIGHT
PLACE ME IN YOUR ARMS HOLD ME TIGHT
WITH THE GENTLENESS OF YOUR HANDS
STROKE MY BREAST
AND LAY MY HEAD UPON YOUR CHEST
THIS LAND OF LOVE WILL ALWAYS BE
THERE OUR SOULS AND MINDS ARE FREE

BEING

BE THE ONE
I CAN'T HIDE
BE THE MAN
WHO'S FILLED WITH PRIDE
BE MY LOVER,
BE MY FRIEND
BE ON MY SIDE
THERE IS NO END
BE IN MY MIND
AND IN MY THOUGHTS
BE FOR ME
THE LOVE I SOUGHT
BE YOURSELF
AND NEVER DEPRIVE
ME OF THE LOVE
YOU HOLD INSIDE
BE THE BIRD
THAT LOVES TO SOAR
AND PLEASE
BE THE LOVE
I'LL HAVE FOREVER MORE

YOU

HERE YOU ARE
A MAN OF SIR-REALITY
SO MUCH OLDER
THAN I EVER COULD BE
TO HAVE YOUTH,
TO BE YOUR LOVER
BEYOND THIS,
YOU WANT NO OTHER
A MAN OF WISDOM WITH NO REAL LOVE
THE SPICES OF LIFE WILL RISE ABOVE
I SEE YOUR GENTLENESS,
PEACE WITHIN
ONLY YOU KNOW WHERE
YOU'RE GOING AT JOURNEYS END
MY FIRST IMPRESSION OF YOU
WAS THAT OF WONDER
A MAN WITHOUT LOVE
IS A MAN LOST
I WANT TO SHARE
A LOVE WITH YOU
IF ONLY FOR JUST A MOMENT

INTERLUDE

TO REST MY MIND IN SOLITUDE
I THINK OF YOU AND OUR INTERLUDE
I HAVE WITHIN MYSELF A BURNING FIRE
WHICH ONLY YOU CAN FILL WITH
COMPLETE DESIRE
TO HOLD YOU AND KISS YOU
AND MAKE CRAZY LOVE
I GRANT WITH WARMTH,
AND FREE AS THE DOVE
EACH DAY I AWAIT TO FEEL LOVES FURY
PASS BY THE TIME, YOU; I ALONE AMOR
TRAPPED BY PASSION TO UNFOLD
SATISFACTION
COME LIVE WITH ME
IN MY MIND AND HEART
HERE LOVE CAN BE, AND NEVER APART
EACH TIME I SEE YOU IT'S AS THE FIRST
NERVES START TO RATTLE,
LUST WANTS TO BURST
HOW I SEE YOU, I WISH TO SHOW
WITH SOME LEFT OVER

MINES

IN LOVES AFTER GLOW
TO HAVE YOU MY LOVE,
I WISH TO PROCEED
PROVIDED OUR HEARTS
SHALL NEVER LEAVE

PASSION & PAIN

THE EMOTION I FEEL INSIDE OF ME,
THAT FUNNY KINDA FEELING
THAT WON'T LET ME BE
TURNING AROUND
I ALWAYS SEE YOUR FACE
THE PASSION I HAVE
CAN'T BE REPLACED
PAIN SETS IN WHEN
THERE'S NO BEING WITH YOU
LIFT THIS BURDEN OFF MY BACK,
BY GIVING ME THE
PASSION I'VE ALWAYS LACK.

COME INTO YESTERDAY

NIGHT COMES,
FOLLOW ME HOME
THE PLEASURES WE'D ROAM
STAND HERE CONVINCED ME TO GO
I KNEW MYSELF I HAD TO KNOW
NEVER NON-SATISFIED
FOR THAT NIGHT THE STATEMENT DENIED
COME INTO YESTERDAY,
RELIEVE THE NIGHT
CHAIN MY HEART,
BUT LET ME BE
ALL YOUR LOVE,
HELD IN ME
I WISH TO HOLD YOU
FOR A WHILE TO SHARE LIFE
AS TO TAKE ME
AS YOUR WIFE
YESTERDAY

I DON'T WANT
TO WAIT IN VAIN

STROLLING VISIONS THROUGH MY HEAD
WHILE LYING ALONE IN BED
I THINK OF WONDROUS DREAMS
INVISIONED WITH YOU,
LOVE I'VE SEENED
MY HEART CRIES OUT
TO HAVE YOU HERE
BUT IT OFTEN KNOWS
YOUR LOVE IS NEAR.
I WAIT WITH PATIENCE,
I WAIT WITH PAIN
CAUSE IT'S FOR YOUR LOVE,
I WAIT IN VAIN
CAST THE MOON HIGH
AND THE STARS AT MY FEET
BACK TO WHEN YOU WERE MINE,
LET TIME REPEAT
ALL THOSE YEARS I SEARCHED FOR LOVE
A LOVE YOU'VE PROVEN ME WORTHY OF

DOUBTS

YOU STATED YOU WANT ME,
NOW YOU'RE UNSURE
SEARCH DEEP AT YOUR FEELINGS
DON'T BE OBSCURE
DON'T WALK AWAY,
I SPEAK AGGRESSIVE
I WON'T CHAIN YOU TO ME,
AS OTHERS TRIED
THE CHANGES I GO THROUGH,
I REFUSE TO HIDE
PLEASE EXPLAIN TO ME
THE FEARS YOU FEEL
TAKE MY LOVE,
BUT BE FOR REAL
I HAD MAN TO LOVE ME
IT SEEMS IMPOSSIBLE TO DO
INTO LIFE,
FATE BRINGS YOU
NOW IT'S IMPOSSIBLE
FOR YOU TO HAVE
I'M NOT IN LOVE,

MINES

WANTED YOU TO BE
A VERY SPECIAL PART OF ME
AND EVEN NOW
I THINK OF NIGHTS SPENT
FOR THE LOVE GIVEN
I WON'T REMENT
I WANT YOU FOR ETERNITY
LOVERS, IF THOUGHT
WE COULD NEVER BE

I'M SO COOL

I'M SO COOL
I'M NO FOOL
STANDING ON THE CORNER
SHUCK AND JIVE
DRINKING WINE
AND GIVE YOU FIVE
HE AND THE FELLAS
TOKING THAT HERB
USING VILE LANGUAGE ONE NEVER HEARD
DIG THAT SCENE, I GOT TO HAVE IT
STICKING YOU UP,
TO SUPPORT HIS HABIT
GO DOWN THE STREET
WE'RE SHOOTING CRAP
DON'T TOUCH MY MONEY,
YOU'RE BOUND TO GET SLAP
FIGHTING BREAKS OUT, THEN A SHOT
THE "MAN" BUSTS YOU,
ALL YOUR LIFE YOU FAIL
NO ONE TO CALL
TO GET YOU OUT OF JAIL.

CONFIDENTIAL

I THINK OF YOU
CONSTANTLY
AS EACH DAY GOES BY
I WANT TO BE WITH YOU
AND INSIDE I CRY
I CRY
FOR THE LOVE
I FEEL FOR YOU
KNOWING NO OTHER LOVE
WILL EVER DO
NO ONE KNOWS
WHAT I FEEL,
ALL FEELINGS
I KEEP CONCEALED

MARRIED MAN

I WISH TO SHARE
MYSELF WITH YOU
I NEED YOUR LOVIN,
LONG OVERDUE
EACH NIGHT GOES BY
AND I WISH YOU WERE HERE
BUT HERE RECENTLY
LONELINESS I FEAR
I KNOW YOU ARE MARRIED
AND I AM YOUR LOVER
BUT I DESIRE YOU ALSO
THIS WAS LONG DISCOVERED
I NEED TO ASK YOU
COULD YOU LOVE ME,
I'M NOT ASKING FOREVER
JUST FOR THE TIME
WE SHARE TOGETHER.

LEA

A PINK ROSE THAT SMELLS SO SWEET
A DESTINATION FOR LOVE, I MUST MEET
SILENCE IS GOLDEN, PURE, AND RARE
BUT THE LOVE OF YOU, I REFUSE TO SHARE
GOING THROUGH LIFE, AT OUR OWN RISKS
IT'S GOOD TO KNOW, THAT YOU EXIST
PASSIONS THAT BURN,
LIKE THE FIRES OF HELL
MAKING ALL FEELINGS
TAKE OFF AND SAIL
EMOTIONS RISES ABOVE THE CLOUDS
TAKING MORE THAN WHAT IS ALLOWED
MAKING LOVE, THE PASSION AND PAIN
WHAT WE PUT IN IT, WILL REMAIN
WISHING WELL: FOR A SHINING PENNY
FRESH AND NEW
I WILL TREASURE EVERY DAY
AND MOMENT
WITH YOU

HURT

THIS IS A LETTER YOU MAY NEVER GET
MY DAYS ARE LONG
OUTSIDE OF LIFE
WHICH I MUST BE A PART OF
I'M ALONE WITH MYSELF
AND MY THOUGHTS
I CAN'T CONTROL WHAT I FEEL WHEN MY
THOUGHTS ARE ABOUT YOU
I SAY BE STRONG,
CAUSE HE HAS, AND HAD TO BE
TIME DOESN'T GO BACK,
THE WRONG IS DONE
AS TIME GOES, THE HURT GETS BETTER
TO HEAR YOUR VOICE: IT'S SO FAR AWAY
AS CLOSE AS I GET TO YOU:
IT'S ONLY IN MY MIND
IMAGINATION PLACES US INTO EACH
OTHERS ARMS

MEMORIES

STANDING ON THE OUTSIDE LOOKING IN
WE'RE TESTING OUR LOVE,
AS TWO OLD FRIENDS
I'VE ALWAYS BEEN ON THE OUTSIDE
LOOKING AT YOU
WONDERING WILL
HE EVER NOTICE ME TOO?
I HELD YOU SO CLOSE TO ME EVEN NOW,
I DON'T KNOW IF IT WAS RIGHT
I WAS SO AFRAID
FOR WHAT YOU WERE THINKING,
YOU CAME FROM OUT OFNOWHERE
IN A POINT IN MY LIFE WHEN I REALLY
NEEDED SOMEONE
AND NOT KNOWING
THIS WAS WHAT I ALWAYS WANTED
UNTIL YOU
ARRIVED.
SO YOU HELD ME, CARESSED MY BODY
AND SOUL AS IF YOU WERE TO
COMMAND MY EVERY MOVEMENT

MINES

I LIE AWAKE NIGHTS CONFUSED BY THOSE POWERFUL MOMENTS
WHEN WE
LIED TOGETHER, YOU MAKING THE DEEPEST OF LOVE TO ME
THERE WAS NEVER A LOVE MORE STRONGER THAN YOU AND I
SOMEHOW THAT BEAUTIFUL TIME OF ECSTASY SEEMS AS
THOUGH
IT SHOULDN'T HAVE BEEN
TAKE AWAY ALL THE PLEASURES
AND PAIN OF LOVE I FELT IF IT'S
NOT RIGHT, AND MAKE IT LIKE A MEMORY.

ETERNALLY

IT'S FROM THE INSPIRATION
THAT YOU GAVE TO ME
THAT LETS
ME FEEL THE WAY I DO
ALL MY LIFE I THOUGHT THERE WILL ALWAYS BE YOU
TIME IS UNIMPORTANT
WHEN IT COMES TO YOU AND I
IF I ONLY HAVE A MINUTE,
HOUR, DAY, WEEKS, OR MONTHS
WITHIN ALL THIS TIME
THERE WILL NEVER BE ENOUGH FOR ME
WHEN IT COMES TO YOU
AND THIS IS SOMETHING
THAT IS VERY SPECIAL TO ME
I LOVE YOU AND I HOPE YOU LOVE ME,
BUT SOMETIMES TO ME
I GET SO INSECURE ABOUT US
I WISH YOU COULD SEE INSIDE OF ME
MAYBE THEN YOU'LL KNOW
EVERY TIME I SEE YOU
MY HEART BEATS FAST,

MINES

IT'S LIKE MY WHOLE
MEANING FOR BEING
HERE IS FOR YOU
AND WHEN YOU'RE GONE
SO IS THE SUN,
THAT WARM FEELING YOU GIVE ME
EVERYTHING HAS CHANGED
ITS FORM AND MEANING
IF I COULD CONTROL THIS WORLD
I WOULD ALWAYS MAKE SURE
THAT WE WOULD HAVE THE SUN
FILLED WITH WARM FEELINGS,
LOVE AND THE COMFORT OF EACH OTHER

STREET LOVER

HE'S COLD AND CALCULATING
FULL OF MISCHIEF
ALWAYS SEEKING
WHAT NEXT HE CAN POSSESS
HE CAN LOVE WITH THE BEST,
TELLING YOU WHAT
YOU WANT TO HEAR
AND THE THINGS HE SAYS ARE
CAPTIVATING TO THE MIND, YOUR BODY GOES
WILLINGLY; NOT KNOWING THE GROUNDS YOU
MAY TRESPASS.
THE FEELING IS THERE FOR A MINUTE
BUT IT NEVER LAST
THE STREET LOVER HAS NO HEART,
HE DRESSES TO THE OCCASION
AND PLAYS THE PART
PLAYING YOUNG LOVE FOR A FOOL
TREATING YOUNG LOVE
SO MEAN AND CRUEL
HEY BABY, IT'S ONLY YOU I LOVE
SOUNDS SO GOOD AND YOUNG LOVE

GRASPING ON TO EVERY WORD,
THIS IS WHAT STREET LOVER WANTS YOU TO DO
HE WRAPS YOUR HEART IN A BIG BLUE BOX
HOLDING ALL THE KEYS,
AND HAVING ALL THE LOCKS
MAKING LOVE TO YOU
WITH THE DEEPEST OF PASSION
HOLDING YOU TIGHT AFTER IT'S OVER
HE'S ALWAYS THERE
WHEN IT'S THE URGE YOU FEEL
CONVEYING EVERY WISH
YOUR BODY HUNGERS
THE GENTLE TOUCH OF HIS HAND
CARESSING YOUR BODY
LIKE THE SWEET TASTE OF WINE
A STREET LOVER TAKES;
HE TAKES YOUR MIND
HE TAKES YOUR HEART
LEAVING YOU TO DREAM
OF THAT EVERLASTING MOMENT
HELD SO DEEP INSIDE OF YOU.
THE PLEASURE AND PAIN
OF IT ALL MAKES YOUR
RESISTANCE A
T ITS MOST WEAKEST STATE.
STREET LOVER HAS
THE POWER TO DOMINATE
HIS CHARACTER IS THAT
WHICH THERE IS NO ESCAPE
YOUNG LOVE HAS THE WISDOM
TO LOVE THIS STREET LOVER
AND FULFILL THAT BURNING DESIRE
HE HOLDS WITHIN

MINES

AND FOR THIS REASON
AND THIS REASON ALONE
YOUNG LOVE AND STREET LOVER
WILL ALWAYS GO ON
TAKING AND GIVING THE ECSTASY
OF EACH MOMENT ARE
SO PRECIOUS AND DEAR
AND CLOSELY KNITTED BETWEEN THEM,
THAT THE TAKING
AND GIVING BUILDS NO FEAR

MUST IT BE THIS WAY

WHY IS IT WE'RE ALWAYS
TWO WORLD APART
YOU GOING YOUR WAY
AND I'M GOING MINE
NEVER REALLY KNOWING
JUST WHAT WE'LL FIND
NEVER KNOWING WHAT'S GOING ON
FROM DAY TO DAY
EACH OF US NEVER FINDING
THE RIGHT WORDS TO SAY
AS WE CROSS EACH OTHERS PATH
SHOWING NOTHING BUT ANGER
AND WRATH
BECAUSE THERE'S NO FUTURE IN THE PAST
JUST PAIN AND MISERY
THAT WILL ALWAYS LAST
BUT WE MUST FIND A WAY
TO SHARE OUR TRUST
TO CONSERVE OUR LOVE
INSTEAD OF FIGHT AND FUSS
FOR AS SURELY AS THERES A GOD ABOVE

MINES

WE MUST FIND A WAY TO SAVE OUR LOVE
OR SHOULD TO EACH OTHER
A LINE SHOULD WE SELL
LET IT BE KNOWN
THE STAR I SOUGHT HAS FELL

HUMAN NATURE

YOU ATTRACT ME IN A FASCINATING WAY
I WAIT AND WONDER
WHEN WILL BE THE DAY
I CAN GET THE CHANCE TO HOLD YOU
AND MAKE DREAMS COME TRUE
THE MAN I WANT I SEE IN YOU
TALL, DARK, AND HANDSOME
AND A REWARDING SMILE
GETTING NEXT TO YOU
WILL TAKE A WHILE
RIGHT NOW I KNOW
YOU'RE NOT LOOKING FOR
ANYTHING SERIOUS
BUT, IMAGINE ME NOT HAVING YOU
AND I GET DELIRIOUS
THERE WILL COME A DAY
WHEN I UP AND TAKE YOUR LOVE AWAY
UNTIL THEN I'LL TAKE IT SLOW
YOU'RE THE ONE I WISH TO KNOW.

ALONE

TO BE SHELTERED IN
NEVER GETTING OUT
I'M LOST AND ALONE
HAVING SOME DOUBT
NO ONE TO SHARE MY BLESSING AND WOE
TO LOVE MY BODY AND TOUCH MY SOUL
IT'S DARK AND EMPTY THAT'S A FRIGHT
NO ONE TO SAY I LOVE YOU
AND KISS GOODNIGHT
CAN'T THANK YOU
FOR THE LOVE YOU BROUGHT
NOT EVEN SHARE A SUDDLE THOUGHT
CONDITIONS PROVED NEVER WORSEN
DEFINITION MEANS WITHOUT
ANY OTHER PERSON
TO BE ALONE

THE CHALLENGE

TO
MAINTAIN YOUR COOL
WHEN OTHERS ARE CRUEL
TO STAY ON TOP,
WHEN IT'S ALL COME DOWN
TO FIGHT FOR WHAT'S RIGHT,
ALL THE WAY AROUND
TO
CARE AND BE KIND
AND UNDERSTAND OTHERS
BLACK OR WHITE
WE
MUST REMAIN SISTERS AND BROTHERS
IN A WORLD WHERE THE ODDS ARE AGAINST YOU
IT'S A
CHALLENGE
WE DO WHAT WE MUST DO

MY PLEDGE

I PLEDGE TO YOU, MY LOVE; AND THAT,
WE'RE BROUGHT TOGETHER
AS ONE, UNITED IN A MUTUAL BOND
I PLEDGE TO YOU, TO BE IN YOUR CORNER, TO BE DEVOTED
LOYAL AND LOVING TO GOD AND YOU,
PUTTING NO OTHERS BEFORE
I PLEDGE TO YOU, TO SHARE MY LIFE
FOR AS LONG AS I SHALL LIVE
TO BE WITH AND BESIDE YOU
I PLEDGE TO YOU, TO DEVOTE MY LIFE PLEASING,
UNDERSTANDING
SHARING AND NEVER LET NO MAN OR WOMAN PUT US UNDER
I PLEDGE: I'M IN YOUR CORNER

ANOTHER CHANCE

IF I COULD HAVE ANOTHER CHANCE
TO LIVE MY LIFE AGAIN
OH THE CHANGES I WOULD MAKE
IN SPITE OF ALL THE PAIN
BUT SINCE I HAVE BUT ONE LIFE TO LIVE
IN THE TIME THAT I'VE BEEN GIVEN
I'LL TRUST IN GOD TO DO HIS WILL
AND ASK TO BE FORGIVEN
I'LL TAKE A CLOSER WALK
WITH HIM WHO DIED UPON THE CROSS
AND PRAY TO HIM MORE OFTEN,
SO TIME WILL NOT BE LOST
I'LL SPREAD THE GOSPEL WHERE I CAN
SO OTHERS KNOW MY LORD
AND TRY TO DO HIS BIDDING
SPENDING MORE IN THE WORD
IF I CAN HAVE THIS ONE MORE CHANCE
TO FOLLOW HIS LEADS
I WILL BE EVER THANKFUL,
IN THOUGHTS, IN WORDS, IN DEEDS.

-S-L-I-C-K-

I DON'T KNOW WHY YOU STAY ON MY MIND
I'LL SEARCH THE WORLD
AND A REASON I CAN'T FIND
IT HURTS ME TO KNOW
YOU REALLY DON'T CARE
TO TRUST ONE WOMAN WITH YOUR LOVE,
YOU DON'T DARE
I CRY ON THE INSIDE
FOR WANTNG YOU SO BAD
THE WAY I FEEL IT'S DRIVING ME MAD
I'M NOT IN LOVE,
BUT I'M FASCINATED BY YOU
I'M CAUGHT IN TWO WORLDS
NOT KNOWING WHAT TO DO
I WON'T GIVE UP ON YOU
THE NEED IS TOO STRONG
I'LL BE PATIENT AND WAIT FOR YOU
NO MATTER HOW LONG
SO MANY WOMEN YOU HAVE
AND YET YOU'RE LONELY
YOU FAIL TO REALIZE I'M LONELY TOO

MINES

THAT MAY BE THE REASON
I'M ATTRACTED TO YOU
YOUR DUCKING AND DODGING
WILL NOT WORK
I'M GOING TO STAY BY YOU
I GUESS I'M A JERK
I CALL YOU UP,
BUT YOU'RE) NEVER HOME, AND
WHEN YOU ARE IT'S OFF WITH THE PHONE
YOUR EYES SHINE BRIGHT IN MY MIND
YOU SMILE SO REAL, YOU'RE NOT MINE
WITH SO MANY WOMEN
YOU NEVER HAVE TIME
MY DAY WILL COME THEN YOU'LL SEE
THAT THE ONLY WOMAN
YOU MAY EVER WANT
JUST MIGHT BE ME

TEMPTATIONS

ALL ALONE JUST YOU AND I
AND NEITHER ONE WONDERS WHY
YOU CAME TO BE LIKE A BALL OF FLAME
AND BEFORE I KNEW IT, I WAS PLAYING YOUR GAME
YOU AND I KNOW THERE'S ANOTHER GIRL
AND I'M JUST NOT A PART OF YOUR WORLD
TO SHARE LOVE AS WE OFTEN DO
IS OH SO FINE, WHEN IT'S ME AND YOU
TWO IS COMPANY, THREE IS A CROWD
IT'S NOTHING TO BE REPEATED OUT LOUD
WE'RE GOOD TOGETHER
AND THAT'S A FACT
BUT PRIDE AND FEELINGS WE OFTEN LACK
SO NOW IT'S TIME
FOR PARTING OF THE WAYS
WE NOW SIT BACK
AND REMEMBER THE DAYS
TIME TO BRING THIS AFFAIR TO AN END
AND ONCE AGAIN I CALL YOU FRIEND
I'M GLAD YOU NOTICED ME

LOVE UP AND MOVED AWAY

IF LOVE UP AND MOVED AWAY
THERE BE NO REASON FOR ANOTHER DAY
THE SUN WOULDN'T SHINE,
THE BIRDS WOULDN'T SING
AND NO JOY WOULD IT BRING
IF LOVE UP AND MOVED AWAY
THERE'S NO REASON FOR YOU TO STAY
THERE WOULD BE NO WILL AND NO WAY
IF LOVE UP AND MOVED AWAY
THE PARK WOULD BE EMPTY
THE SKY WOULD BE GREY
IF LOVE UP AND MOVED AWAY
THE EARTH WOULDN'T HOLD
A PRECIOUS LOVE,
THERE BE NO FULFILLMENT OF DREAMS
NO BEAUTY OF THE DOVE.
NO PICTURE OF PRETTY SCHEME
IF LOVE UP AND MOVED AWAY
THE LOVE I FEEL WOULD NEVER STAY

-S-L-I-C-K-

WHAT TYPE OF WOMAN INTEREST YOU,
MUST SHE BE TALL OR SHORT
WHICH WILL DO
DOES SHE HAVE TO BE WITTY
OR JUST SO PLAIN
WHICH WILL CONQUER,
WHICH WILL GAIN
WILL LONG HAIR OR SHORT HAIR
MAKE THE DIFFERENCE
OR ARE WE NOT GOING BY APPEARANCE
IS IT THE FACT THAT HER EYES ARE
BROWN OR BLACK
OR IS IT THE EXPERIENCE
SHE MUSTN'T LACK
SHALL HER NAME BE "ANGEL"
OR A "DEVILISH BITCH"
WHICH WILL YOU CHOOSE
TO MAKE A HITCH
SHOULD SHE BE OBESE OR SLENDER
TO CATCH YOUR EYE
OR DOES IT MATTER

84

AFTER THE WORD "GOOD-BYE"
CHARM AND POISE ARE OFTEN THE KEY
WHEN LOVE MAKING OCCURS
THAT'S WHERE YOU'LL BE
MAYBE NONE OF THESE THINGS
MAY INTEREST YOU
THE FACT SHE'S A WOMAN ALONE WILL DO

SUMMER SONNET

HATE ME NOT FOR WHAT I DO
BUT UNDERSTAND IT'S BECAUSE OF YOU
DEDICATE YOURSELF
FOR WHAT YOU BELIEVE
I'LL BE LOYAL
WITH EVERY BREATH I BREATHE
LOVE ME FOR THE THINGS I SAY
HOLD ME TIGHT, DON'T PUSH AWAY
COME INTO MY HEART,
WELCOME WITH OPEN ARMS
TAKE MY HAND LET'S WALK
TOGETHER SHARING LOVE
TAKE AWAY; IF YOU MUST, DEEPEST DESIRE
STILL HAVING YOU TO HOLD
FOR STRENGTH GOES ON,
TAKE ME TO A WINTERS DOVE
AND ALWAYS RETURN ME
MY SUMMER'S LOVE

A-LONG PAST TIME

A LONG PAST TIME, AND SO MANY YEARS
A LONG PAST TIME,
OF MEMORY AND TEARS
A LONG PAST TIME,
FOR YOU AND I
A LONG PAST TIME, IT MADE ME CRY
A LONG PAST TIME, I THOUGHT WE MEET
A LONG PAST TIME,
THE RACE OF MY HEARTBEAT
A LONG PAST TIME,
I THOUGHT I'D LOSE YOU
A LONG PAST TIME, I FELT THE WAY I DO
A LONG PAST TIME, OF MEMORIES GONE BY
A LONG PAST TIME, AND I STILL CRY
A LONG PAST TIME,
OF THE MEMORY OF A MAN
I WAS SO IN LOVE WITH
A LONG PAST TIME,
THE LOVE THAT WAS GIVEN
I'LL NEVER FORGET.

LOVE

IF YOU LOVE ME, WHY WON'T YOU STAY
YOU MAKE LOVE TO ME
AND LEAVE ME THIS WAY
MY EMOTIONS ARE WEAK
AND YOU'RE MY STRENGTH
BUT OUR LOVE HAS BEEN TESTED
TO ITS LENGTH
I WANT TO SHOW YOU
I'LL ALWAYS CARE,
BUT CAN YOU PROMISE ME
YOU'LL ALWAYS BE THERE
I'LL GIVE TO YOU MY ALL IN ALL
EVERY TIME I SEE YOU
DEEPER IN LOVE I FALL
CALL BACK THE HANDS OF TIME,
BACK WHEN I REMEMBER YOU WERE MINE
STROLLING THROUGH LIFE
SO LOVING AND CAREFREE
AND YOU WILL BE
THAT SPECIAL PART OF ME
YOU CAN TAKE ALL YOU WANT FROM ME

MINES

WHEN IT COMES TO LOVE
BECAUSE MY ALL IS REALLY NOT ENOUGH
YOU CAN FILL THIS EMPTINESS
IN MY HEART
LETS STAY FOREVER
IN LOVE AND NEVER APART

A MAN OF

A MAN OF BEAUTY
A MAN OF GRACE
A MAN WITH DIGNITY,
WRITTEN ON HIS FACE
A MAN OF PRIDE
A MAN OF STYLE
A MAN OF WISDOM HE CANNOT HIDE
A MAN OF FEELING
A MAN OF MEN
A MAN OF LOVE
MUCH MORE REVEALING
A MAN OF BEAUTY
AND A MAN OF GRACE
A MAN OF MANY
NEVER TO BE REPLACED

STARFIRE

THE WAY I FEEL TONIGHT
THAT FOREVER FEELING,
I KNOW IT'S RIGHT
THOU, NOTHING CAN STOP ME
FROM FEELING LIKE I DO
I LOOK AT THE STARS
AND THERE'S ALWAYS YOU
THE STARS ARE ON FIRE,
AND THEY'RE BURNING WITH
THE WORLD'S DESIRE
TWINKLING IN A BLUE SKY,
LOOKS SO AT PEACE
NEVER HAVING TO KNOW
THE PLEASURE AND THE PAIN
OF LIFE AND LOVE
AT NIGHT THE STARS MAKE MUSIC
AND THE MOON
PUTS A LIGHT
ON THEM.
THAT LETS THE WORLD SEE
THE STARS IN SYMPHONY

MINES

SINGING ON BEHALF OF ALL LOVERS
EACH NIGHT IT FILLS YOU
WITH A BURNING DESIRE
AND THE STARS KNOW,
CAUSE THEY'RE ON FIRE.

AUGUST

THE DAYS ARE LONG,
I CAN'T REMEMBER THE LAST TIME
I'VE FELT THE TOUCH OF LOVE
MY LOVE DIDN'T BELONG,
I DID IN FACT CALL YOU
THROUGH MY MIND
LATER YOU APPEARED,
SUDDENLY YOU DISAPPEARED
JUST LIKE YOU CAME FROM A THOUGHT
WE TOUCH BY NIGHT
GONE UNTIL THE TIME THE NEED IS RIGHT
MY HOW THE TIME FLIES
WHEN YOU'RE HAVING FUN.

LET YOUR MIND WONDER

LET YOUR MIND WONDER FOR A MINUTE,
NOW THINK OF ALL
THE GOOD THINGS YOU KNOW.
WHEN I LET MY MIND WONDER
I THINK OF ONE MANS LOVE
THE TOUCH OF HIS HANDS,
WHEN HE CARESSES MY BODY
THE THINGS HE SAYS
THAT LETS MY MIND BE FREE
HIS BOYISH WAYS AND HIS WINNING SMILE,
AND WHEN WE'RE
IN BED, I LOVE HIS STYLE.
ALL THE GOOD THINGS
I KNOW IS THE HAPPINESS
THIS ONE MAN HAS BROUGHT ME.
IT'S PARADISE
AND THERE'S NOTHING WRONG.
THE LONG WALKS IN THE PARK, WHERE WE CAN LET OURSELVES
GO
FREE AND LOVING.
WHEN I LET MY MIND WONDER

MINES

I THINK OF THE TEACHINGS OF HIS
LOVE AND OF HIS MIND.
I LET MY MIND WONDER
AND I THINK!!!
A MINUTE IS UP

PRIVATE FEELINGS

THROUGHOUT LIFE WE LEARN TO GROW
AND THERE'S TWO THINGS
WE ALL SHOULD KNOW
LIFE IS COMPLICATED AND LOVE IS HARD
WE GO THROUGH LIFE
NOT KNOWING WHERE TO START
WE LEARN TO GROW
IN A ATMOSPHERE OF SOLITUDE
WHERE THE WORLD IS HARSH,
HEARTBROKEN, AND CRUEL
MAN AND WOMAN
WERE BROUGHT TOGETHER UNITE AS ONE
BUT MAN'S CRUELTY
OF HUMAN LOVE HAS WON
IF IN TIME WE CAN KNOW
WHAT WE SEEK IN THIS WORLD
OF DISCREET LOVE AND PAIN,
ALL THE DREAMS OF HAPPINESS
WON'T CHANGE

RITUALS

SOMETIMES IN OUR LIFE
WE INHERIT TROUBLE AND STRIFE
BUT THE GOOD WILL PREVAIL
WHEN ALL ELSE FAILS
SO KEEP YOUR HEAD HIGH
AND DON'T ALWAYS ASK WHY
BECAUSE ONLY THE LORD KNOWS
WHY THIS IS THE WAY
THAT THE WIND SHALL BLOW
PRAY TO HIM TO KEEP YOU STRONG
THEN IN HIM YOU'LL NEVER GO WRONG

US

I CAME THIS FAR TO BE WITH YOU,
THROUGH THE GOOD TIMES AND
THE BAD.
LOVE MADE SO BEAUTIFULLY
IN THE SWEETEST SPLENDOR.
SEARCHING TO FIND IN EACH OTHER
THE DEPTH OF LOVE AND
UNDERSTANDING, AND BELIEVE
THAT LOVE IS GREATER
I GAVE TO YOU MY ALL AND ALL,
YOU GIVE TO ME YOUR DEVOTION
TOGETHER WE PLANT A SEED
THAT WILL GROW TO BE
AND IT'S OBVIOUS IT WAS MEANT TO BE

DEVILISH BITCH

TO CHEAT, STEAL, AND CONNIVE
COME TO YOUR FACE AND TELL YOU LIES
PLAYING YOU UP AS A LOVE SO TRUE
TRICKS OF THE TRADE ARE NEVER KNEW
SATISFIES HER LOVER
IN A COLD CALLOUS WAY
SPINNING A WEB FOR THE GAME SHE PRAY
BODY IN GOOD FORMATION
AND CURVES JUST RIGHT
EYES OF A COBRA AND A DEADLY BITE
DOMINATE EMOTIONS
TO THE FULLEST MEASURE
SEEING YOU SUFFER GIVES HER PLEASURE
BY FAR NO MAN WOULD WANT THIS
TO BE HIS LOVER
BUT SHE'S SO FINE ON THE OUTSIDE
TOO DEEP TO DISCOVER
DON'T LET HER RIDE DOWN ON YOU,
YOU'LL HIT THE DITCH
THIS LADY IS BAD AND A DEVILISH BITCH

EVE

ON THIS NIGHT OF LOVE AND SPLENDOR
TO YOU MY LOVE I DO SURRENDER
THE JOY I FOUND CAN'T BE REPLACED
BUT NOW YOU'RE GONE WITHOUT A TRACE
IN MY HEART I'D THOUGHT IT'LL BE
ME FOR YOU AND YOU FOR ME
I LOVED YOU THEN, AND I LOVE YOU NOW
YOU LOOK IN MY EYES AND ASK ME HOW
IT WAS YEARS AGO I SWORE DEVOTION
NOW THE WHEELS OF TIME
ARE MOVING IN MOTION
WHEN YOU HELD ME IN YOUR ARMS
AND HELD ME TIGHT
I FELT YOUR LOVE AND I HAD TO FIGHT
DEEP DOWN IN YOUR HEART
I DON'T KNOW HOW YOU FEEL
BUT DEEP DOWN IN MINE
THE LOVE IS REAL
NIGHTS ARE IMPOSSIBLE TO SLEEP ALONE
WAITING FOR THE RING OF THE PHONE
I CRY AND I PRAY THAT YOU'LL FIND A WAY
YOU BASE LOVE ON THE MATERIAL THINGS
WHEN LOVE IS THE JOY THAT IT BRINGS.

RENAISSANCE

NOW THE TIME HAS COME FOR US
TO GO OUR SEPARATE WAYS
NO MORE LONG NIGHT
BLISS OF ROMANTIC DAYS
THOU, I FEEL THE WAY I DO
I KNOW YOU CAN'T HELP BUT FEEL IT TOO
NO MORE DAYS OF PLEASURE AND PAIN
ONLY STRENGTH WILL HAVE TO GAIN
TIME WAITS FOR NO MAN
AS YOU CAN SURELY SEE
THERE WASN'T ENOUGH TIME
FOR YOU AND ME
IT WAS HARD GIVING YOU UP
I DRANK BITTER TEA FROM MY LOVIN CUP
SO NO HARD FEELINGS AS FAR AS IT GO
CAUSE BABY THE NEXT TIME I'LL KNOW
I HAVEN'T LOST YOU
I'VE GAINED MY FREEDOM

WARM THOUGHTS

I REMEMBER THE LOVE SHARED
THE WAY YOU HELD ME, AS WE LIE IN BED
WALK IN THE PARK TO MAKE LOVE IN THE DARK
WAKING UP, FINDING YOU THERE
BY MY SIDE, WITH LOVE AND CARE
A WARM BATH FOR YOU MY LOVE,
SOFT CANDLELIGHT
SOOTHING MUSIC, TO MAKE IT RIGHT
WE'VE SHARED SO MUCH,
REMEMBER THE IMPORTANCE
TO KNOW WHAT LOVE IS;
AND LOVE IT, THOSE PRECIOUS
MOMENTS IN LIFE
I MAY NEVER AGAIN GIVE
LOVE SO TRUE FULFILLY LIVED
ANOTHER THOUGHT CAN NEVER DO
THESE ARE THE WARM THOUGHTS OF YOU

CAPTURED

WHEN I SEE YOU
SOMETHING INSIDE ME STIRRED
HAVE YOU HEARD
IT WAS LIKE SEEING YOU
FOR THE VERY FIRST TIME
AND ALL THAT WHILE
YOU WERE STILL MINE
IF NIGHT WAS DAY AND DAY WAS NIGHT
WOULD THIS FEELING BE OH SO RIGHT
THOUGH WE'RE MANY MILES APART
I STILL HOLD YOU IN MY HEART
AND AS TIME GOES BY SO SLOW
I WANT YOU HERE AND THIS YOU KNOW
YOU NEED YOUR SPACE
AND IT HAS ITS PLACE
DON'T MAKE THAT SPACE INFINITY
THAT GAP IS TOO BIG TO BE
YOU STEPPED INTO MY LIFE AND MADE IT BEAUTIFUL
MAKING ME FEEL WANTED
TAKE AWAY ALL THE TREASURES OF THE WORLD
AND LEAVE ME YOU AND MY SONNET.

MY LOVE

WHEN I CLOSE MY EYES I THINK OF YOU
AND ALL THE THINGS WE'VE YET TO DO
WHAT I NEED IS TO HAVE YOU HERE
WHILE YOU ARE FAR AND STILL SO NEAR
WHERE TIME IS DISTANT
AND IT'S JUST US TWO
I REMAIN EMPTY, AND LONG FOR YOU
WHY MUST I HURT FOR THE LOVE OF YOU
WILD PASSION OF DESIRE BRINGS XANADAU
HOW LONG MUST I WAIT FOR MY LOVE
I BRING FORTH TO YOU A GIFT FILLED WITH
RESPECT, KINDNESS, AND WISDOM
CONTAINED IN THE LITTLE BOX, BARES
THE WORLDS MOST
PRECIOUS GIFT, I GIVE YOU LOVE

DISTANT

I WANT TO BE WITH YOU ONE ON ONE
BUT YOU'RE AS CLOSE TO ME
AS THE DISTANT SUN
WHEN I APPROACH THE PLACE,
I KNOW WE'LL MEET
I'LL SAY HELLO, AND STAY ON MY FEET
BUT IN ACTUALITY I WISH TO TAKE YOU
AND HOLD YOU TIGHT
AND I DREAD THE TIME
YOU SAY GOODNIGHT
BUT CIRCUMSTANCES PREVAILS
US TO STAY APART
AND I SEE IN YOUR EYES
WHAT I FEEL, IN MY HEART
AS TIME GOES BY, WE'LL LEARN TO GROW
ENJOYING EACH OTHER
ONE THING THAT I'VE NOTICED OF YOU,
A MAN OF LITTLE WORDS
BUT THIS FOR ME IS NO CONCERN
THE ONLY THING I NEED TO SEE
YOUR WARM SMILE, SMILING BACK AT ME

MINES

THE DAY WILL COME AND WE'LL NO
LONGER MEET IN THIS PLACE
AS IT SHALL ALSO TELL
OF AMAZING GRACE

UNCERTAIN MEANING

TAKE PITY ON ME,
FOR I WAS BLIND AND COULDN'T SEE
THAT YOUR LOVE WASN'T MEANT TO BE
TAKE PITY ON ME,
FOR THE THINGS I'VE DONE
I ONCE HAD YOU AND NOW YOU'RE GONE
WE MOVED SO FAST
NOT KNOWING WHERE WE WERE GOING
AND NOW WE'RE THERE
WE CROSS BOUNTY LINES,
WHEN NO ONE DARE
WE'RE NOT IN LOVE,
WE'RE LONELY AND ALONE
OH, WHAT'S THE USE
ME SITTING HERE THINKING UP AN EXCUSE
I GAVE UP MYSELF
AS A SACRIFICE JUST TO FILL
THE EMPTINESS
IN BOTH OUR LIVES
SO NOW I'M LOST
AND YOU ARE TOO,

MINES

AND NEITHER KNOWS WHAT TO DO
WE DIDN'T GIVE EACH OTHER
ENOUGH TIME TO DECIDE
BUT RUNNING FROM OUR LONELINESS, WE HAVE TO HIDE
I DON'T NEED PITY IN THAT WAY,
I NEED A FRIEND TO COUNT ON
FROM DAY TO DAY
AND IF IT'S PITY YOU FEEL FOR ME
THEN I AM THROUGH
CAUSE IT'S THE SAME PITY I FEEL FOR YOU.

NEEDS

I NEED YOUR STRENGTH
TO PROTECT ME FROM THE STORM
I NEED YOUR LOVE
TO KEEP ME SAFE AND WARM
I NEED YOUR ARMS TO HOLD ME TIGHT
I NEED YOUR BODY TO LIE BY AT NIGHT
I NEED YOUR LIPS PRESSED UPON MINE
I NEED THE LOVE, I HOPED WE'LL FIND
I NEED THE LORD TO STAND BY ME
AND PLACE MY LIFE TO TRUST IN THEE
BUT MOST OF ALL I NEED TO HAVE YOU
TO NEVER SAY THIS LOVE IS THROUGH
SUCH ARE THE NEEDS I HAVE
I CAN NEVER CONQUER
FOR IT'S THE REASON
OF MY EXISTING HUNGER
FOR YOU ARE MY LOVE
WE'LL PLANT THIS SEED
FROM YOU,
THESE ARE THE THINGS I NEED

GOLDEN BOY

Dedicated to Milford Dunn

WITH WINGS A SWIFT AND GOLDEN EMBER
COME TO ME, I DO SURRENDER
DESIRES THAT BURN LIKE THE FIRES OF HELL
TAKE ME NOW I WILL AVAIL
MAKING LOVE TO ME,
PLEASE HELP TO DEFINE
THE GENTLE GOLDEN TOUCH
YOU MAKE REFINE
GOLDEN BOY WITH EYES OF TRUST
OF PASSIONS FOR YOU I MORTALLY LUST
STAY WITH ME TO ACHIEVE AND GAIN
THE GOLDEN LOVE I SOUGHT TO REMAIN
AND WHEN MIDNIGHT FALLS
THEN WE'LL UNITE
WITH A GOLDEN LOVE
NOT PLACED BY SIGHT
FOR THIS IS TO BE MY ULTIMATE GOAL
TO HAVE IN YOU
THE LOVE I HOLD . . .
GOLDEN BOY